The Nature Notebook Series

Edited By

ANNA BOTSFORD COMSTOCK

The Bird Notebook

By

ANNA BOTSFORD COMSTOCK

OUTLINES OF BIRDS

BY

LOUIS AGASSIZ FUERTES

BOOK NO. 1

THIS 6"X9" EDITION PUBLISHED 2021
BY LIVING BOOK PRESS
IN ASSOCIATION WITH
HEARTHROOM PRESS

ILLUSTRATIONS BY: LOUIS AGASSIZ FUERTES

ORIGINAL WORK PUBLISHED 1913
BY
THE COMSTOCK PUBLISHING COMPANY

FOR MORE INFORMATION, CONTACT:
HEARTHROOM PRESS
INFO@HEARTHROOMPRESS.COM

ISBN: 987-1-922348-79-1

NATIONAL
LIBRARY
OF AUSTRALIA

A catalogue record for this
book is available from the
National Library of Australia

This notebook is planned to combine schoolroom work with field observations. The notes should be begun in the field and may be completed by consulting bird books. The outlines of the birds should be colored in the schoolroom or at home since they need to be detailed with care.

Wherever it is possible, underscore the words of the question to indicate the answer. For instance, if the bird is seen in the woods then underscore the word "woods," This will save time. In observing birds it is necessary to learn to look quickly and see accurately one or two characteristics of the bird, since it rarely sits still or patiently to wait for slow observation. Look first for the general color, then for the colors of the back, breast, wings and tail, and when the bird is flying note if it shows colors. As soon as the observation is made, record it in the book. Flash colors are usually white and they show only when the bird is flying. These patches of lighter color are supposed to help keep the flock together during night migrations, and they are supposed to be protective. For example, if a hawk were after a meadow lark while that bird was flying, it would notice the white feathers in the tail; but as soon as the meadow-lark alighted the white would disappear and the hawk would be puzzled. The robin has some very interesting flash colors. Although space for the name of the bird is placed first in the notes, this may be the last thing added. It should not be written until the observer is certain of the species. The outlines of the birds were drawn by Louis Agassiz Fuertes and include fifty-eight common to the Eastern United States. Thirty of the more common appear in Notebook No. 1 and twenty-eight in Notebook No. 2. These outlines may be colored from the observations made in the field and recorded in the notes; or they may be colored from pictures. The first plan has the quality of entirely original work, while the latter has the advantage of making the observer familiar with the markings of the bird and thus is of great assistance in enabling him to recognize the bird in the field. [For copy to follow in coloring the birds, Farmers' bulletin 513 of the United States Department of Agriculture is entitled, "Fifty Common Birds of Farm and Orchard" is especially excellent. The colored pictures of birds issued by the Perry Company may also be used for copy; the illustrations in, "Bird Neighbors," "Birds that Hunt and are Hunted,"by Neltje Blanchan, and "The Bird Guide part 2" by Chester A. Reed and in the Audubon Leaflets will prove useful for copying.] As many notes should be taken in the field as is possible; if the questions are not all answered during one excursion, they may be finished at some other time. Absolute accuracy is essential in the bird observation.

INDEX TO BIRD NOTES

INDEX TO BIRD NOTES

Name of Bird	Page

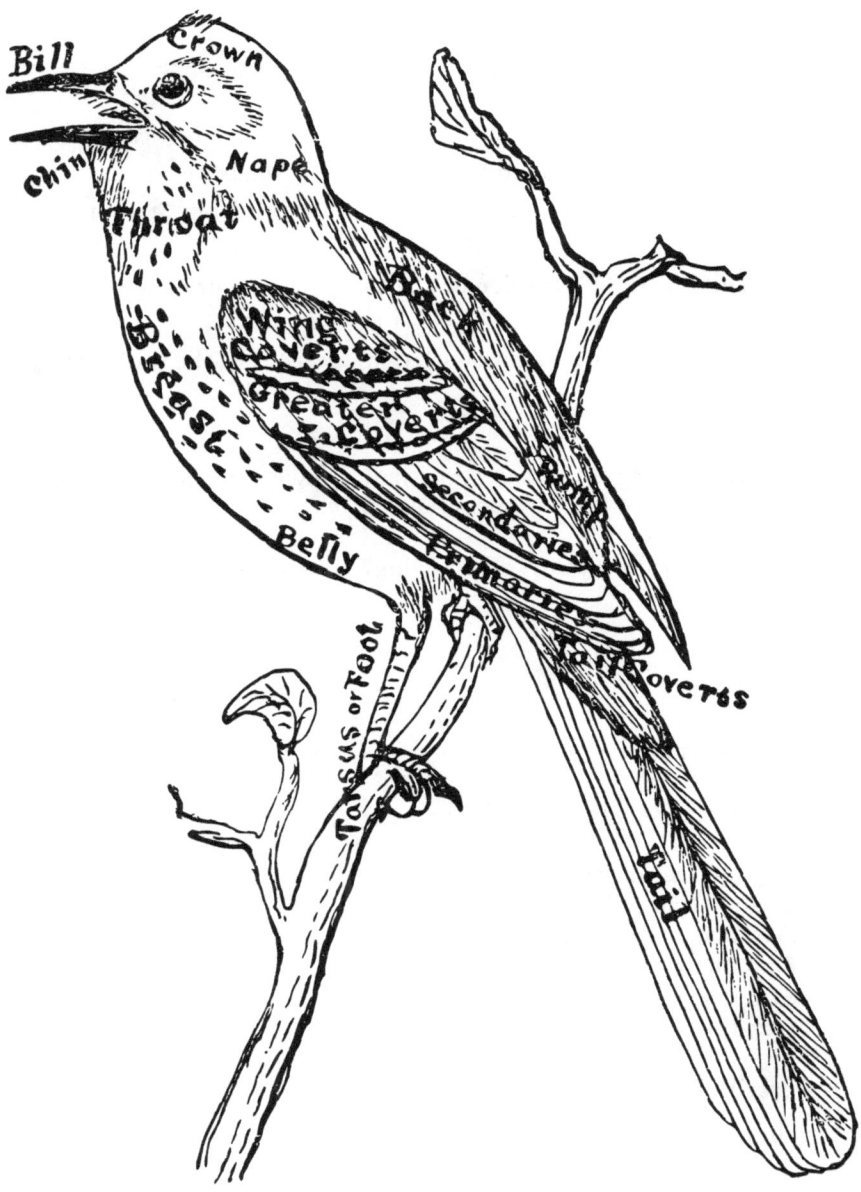

Bill

Crown

Chin

Nape

Throat

Breast

Back

Wing
coverts

greater
coverts

Belly

secondaries

rump

Primaries

tail coverts

Tarsus or Foot

Tail

UNDERSCORE THE WORDS WHICH DESCRIBE THE BIRD

Date:

Name of Bird: See Picture, page:

1. Where is the bird seen :

Woods	Open Field	Roadsides
Border of Woods	Trees	Border of Stream
Bushes	Along Fences	Marsh
About Buildings	Garden or Orchard	Pond or Lake

2. Compare the size of the bird with that of the crow, the robin, or the English Sparrow.

3. Its most striking colors are: Gray, slate, brown, chestnut, black, white, blue, red, yellow, orange, green, olive.

4. Does it show flash colors when flying? If so what color?
   Wing:
   Rump:
   Tail:
   Under Tail:

5. In action is it: Slow and quiet or active and nervous?

6. Does it occur alone or in a flock?

7. In flying does it go:
   Straight and swift
   Dart about Up and down wave-like
   Flap the wings constantly
   Sail or soar with wings steady
   Flap the wings and then sail

8. Describe its song or call note?

9. Where does it sit when singing? Does it sing when flying?

FOR CLOSER OBSERVATION

10. Colors and markings of:

Breast: Top of head:

Wings: Eye streak:

Tail: Back:

11. Is the bill: Slender and long, short and thick, medium, curved, hooked?

12. Is the tail: Forked, notched, square, rounded?

THE FOLLOWING QUESTIONS SHOULD BE ANSWERED FROM OBSERVATION, IF POSSIBLE; IF NOT, THE ANSWER MAY BE FOUND BY CONSULTING BIRD BOOKS.

13. What is the food of the bird and how obtained?

14. Where does the bird spend the winter?

15. Describe the nest, where placed, how far from the ground, how supported, of what material is the outside made, how lined? The color and number of eggs.

16. How are the young fed and cared for? The colors of plumage of the young birds?

17. Is the bird beneficial to us, and if so, how and why?

UNDERSCORE THE WORDS WHICH DESCRIBE THE BIRD

Date:

Name of Bird: See Picture, page:

1. Where is the bird seen :

Woods	Open Field	Roadsides
Border of Woods	Trees	Border of Stream
Bushes	Along Fences	Marsh
About Buildings	Garden or Orchard	Pond or Lake

2. Compare the size of the bird with that of the crow, the robin, or the English Sparrow.

3. Its most striking colors are: Gray, slate, brown, chestnut, black, white, blue, red, yellow, orange, green, olive.

4. Does it show flash colors when flying? If so what color?
    Wing:
    Rump:
    Tail:
    Under Tail:

5. In action is it: Slow and quiet or active and nervous?

6. Does it occur alone or in a flock?

7. In flying does it go:
    Straight and swift
    Dart about Up and down wave-like
    Flap the wings constantly
    Sail or soar with wings steady
    Flap the wings and then sail

8. Describe its song or call note?

9. Where does it sit when singing? Does it sing when flying?

FOR CLOSER OBSERVATION

10. Colors and markings of:

Breast: Top of head:

Wings: Eye streak:

Tail: Back:

11. Is the bill: Slender and long, short and thick, medium, curved, hooked?

12. Is the tail: Forked, notched, square, rounded?

THE FOLLOWING QUESTIONS SHOULD BE ANSWERED FROM OBSERVATION, IF POSSIBLE; IF NOT, THE ANSWER MAY BE FOUND BY CONSULTING BIRD BOOKS.

13. What is the food of the bird and how obtained?

14. Where does the bird spend the winter?

15. Describe the nest, where placed, how far from the ground, how supported, of what material is the outside made, how lined? The color and number of eggs.

16. How are the young fed and cared for? The colors of plumage of the young birds?

17. Is the bird beneficial to us, and if so, how and why?

UNDERSCORE THE WORDS WHICH DESCRIBE THE BIRD

Date:

Name of Bird: See Picture, page:

1. Where is the bird seen :

Woods	Open Field	Roadsides
Border of Woods	Trees	Border of Stream
Bushes	Along Fences	Marsh
About Buildings	Garden or Orchard	Pond or Lake

2. Compare the size of the bird with that of the crow, the robin, or the English Sparrow.

3. Its most striking colors are: Gray, slate, brown, chestnut, black, white, blue, red, yellow, orange, green, olive.

4. Does it show flash colors when flying? If so what color?
    Wing:
    Rump:
    Tail:
    Under Tail:

5. In action is it: Slow and quiet or active and nervous?

6. Does it occur alone or in a flock?

7. In flying does it go:
    Straight and swift
    Dart about Up and down wave-like
    Flap the wings constantly
    Sail or soar with wings steady
    Flap the wings and then sail

8. Describe its song or call note?

9. Where does it sit when singing? Does it sing when flying?

FOR CLOSER OBSERVATION

10. Colors and markings of:

Breast: Top of head:

Wings: Eye streak:

Tail: Back:

11. Is the bill: Slender and long, short and thick, medium, curved, hooked?

12. Is the tail: Forked, notched, square, rounded?

THE FOLLOWING QUESTIONS SHOULD BE ANSWERED FROM OBSERVATION, IF POSSIBLE; IF NOT, THE ANSWER MAY BE FOUND BY CONSULTING BIRD BOOKS.

13. What is the food of the bird and how obtained?

14. Where does the bird spend the winter?

15. Describe the nest, where placed, how far from the ground, how supported, of what material is the outside made, how lined? The color and number of eggs.

16. How are the young fed and cared for? The colors of plumage of the young birds?

17. Is the bird beneficial to us, and if so, how and why?

UNDERSCORE THE WORDS WHICH DESCRIBE THE BIRD

Date:

Name of Bird: See Picture, page:

1. Where is the bird seen :

Woods	Open Field	Roadsides
Border of Woods	Trees	Border of Stream
Bushes	Along Fences	Marsh
About Buildings	Garden or Orchard	Pond or Lake

2. Compare the size of the bird with that of the crow, the robin, or the English Sparrow.

3. Its most striking colors are: Gray, slate, brown, chestnut, black, white, blue, red, yellow, orange, green, olive.

4. Does it show flash colors when flying? If so what color?
    Wing:
    Rump:
    Tail:
    Under Tail:

5. In action is it: Slow and quiet or active and nervous?

6. Does it occur alone or in a flock?

7. In flying does it go:
    Straight and swift
    Dart about Up and down wave-like
    Flap the wings constantly
    Sail or soar with wings steady
    Flap the wings and then sail

8. Describe its song or call note?

9. Where does it sit when singing? Does it sing when flying?

FOR CLOSER OBSERVATION

10. Colors and markings of:

Breast: Top of head:

Wings: Eye streak:

Tail: Back:

11. Is the bill: Slender and long, short and thick, medium, curved, hooked?

12. Is the tail: Forked, notched, square, rounded?

THE FOLLOWING QUESTIONS SHOULD BE ANSWERED FROM OBSERVATION, IF POSSIBLE; IF NOT, THE ANSWER MAY BE FOUND BY CONSULTING BIRD BOOKS.

13. What is the food of the bird and how obtained?

14. Where does the bird spend the winter?

15. Describe the nest, where placed, how far from the ground, how supported, of what material is the outside made, how lined? The color and number of eggs.

16. How are the young fed and cared for? The colors of plumage of the young birds?

17. Is the bird beneficial to us, and if so, how and why?

UNDERSCORE THE WORDS WHICH DESCRIBE THE BIRD

Date:

Name of Bird: See Picture, page:

1. Where is the bird seen :

Woods	Open Field	Roadsides
Border of Woods	Trees	Border of Stream
Bushes	Along Fences	Marsh
About Buildings	Garden or Orchard	Pond or Lake

2. Compare the size of the bird with that of the crow, the robin, or the English Sparrow.

3. Its most striking colors are: Gray, slate, brown, chestnut, black, white, blue, red, yellow, orange, green, olive.

4. Does it show flash colors when flying? If so what color?
    Wing:
    Rump:
    Tail:
    Under Tail:

5. In action is it: Slow and quiet or active and nervous?

6. Does it occur alone or in a flock?

7. In flying does it go:
    Straight and swift
    Dart about Up and down wave-like
    Flap the wings constantly
    Sail or soar with wings steady
    Flap the wings and then sail

8. Describe its song or call note?

9. Where does it sit when singing? Does it sing when flying?

FOR CLOSER OBSERVATION

10. Colors and markings of:

Breast: Top of head:

Wings: Eye streak:

Tail: Back:

11. Is the bill: Slender and long, short and thick, medium, curved, hooked?

12. Is the tail: Forked, notched, square, rounded?

THE FOLLOWING QUESTIONS SHOULD BE ANSWERED FROM OBSERVATION, IF POSSIBLE; IF NOT, THE ANSWER MAY BE FOUND BY CONSULTING BIRD BOOKS.

13. What is the food of the bird and how obtained?

14. Where does the bird spend the winter?

15. Describe the nest, where placed, how far from the ground, how supported, of what material is the outside made, how lined? The color and number of eggs.

16. How are the young fed and cared for? The colors of plumage of the young birds?

17. Is the bird beneficial to us, and if so, how and why?

UNDERSCORE THE WORDS WHICH DESCRIBE THE BIRD

Date:

Name of Bird: See Picture, page:

1. Where is the bird seen :

Woods	Open Field	Roadsides
Border of Woods	Trees	Border of Stream
Bushes	Along Fences	Marsh
About Buildings	Garden or Orchard	Pond or Lake

2. Compare the size of the bird with that of the crow, the robin, or the English Sparrow.

3. Its most striking colors are: Gray, slate, brown, chestnut, black, white, blue, red, yellow, orange, green, olive.

4. Does it show flash colors when flying? If so what color?
    Wing:
    Rump:
    Tail:
    Under Tail:

5. In action is it: Slow and quiet or active and nervous?

6. Does it occur alone or in a flock?

7. In flying does it go:
    Straight and swift
    Dart about Up and down wave-like
    Flap the wings constantly
    Sail or soar with wings steady
    Flap the wings and then sail

8. Describe its song or call note?

9. Where does it sit when singing? Does it sing when flying?

FOR CLOSER OBSERVATION

10. Colors and markings of:

Breast: Top of head:

Wings: Eye streak:

Tail: Back:

11. Is the bill: Slender and long, short and thick, medium, curved, hooked?

12. Is the tail: Forked, notched, square, rounded?

THE FOLLOWING QUESTIONS SHOULD BE ANSWERED FROM OBSERVATION, IF POSSIBLE; IF NOT, THE ANSWER MAY BE FOUND BY CONSULTING BIRD BOOKS.

13. What is the food of the bird and how obtained?

14. Where does the bird spend the winter?

15. Describe the nest, where placed, how far from the ground, how supported, of what material is the outside made, how lined? The color and number of eggs.

16. How are the young fed and cared for? The colors of plumage of the young birds?

17. Is the bird beneficial to us, and if so, how and why?

UNDERSCORE THE WORDS WHICH DESCRIBE THE BIRD

Date:

Name of Bird: See Picture, page:

1. Where is the bird seen :

Woods	Open Field	Roadsides
Border of Woods	Trees	Border of Stream
Bushes	Along Fences	Marsh
About Buildings	Garden or Orchard	Pond or Lake

2. Compare the size of the bird with that of the crow, the robin, or the English Sparrow.

3. Its most striking colors are: Gray, slate, brown, chestnut, black, white, blue, red, yellow, orange, green, olive.

4. Does it show flash colors when flying? If so what color?
 Wing:
 Rump:
 Tail:
 Under Tail:

5. In action is it: Slow and quiet or active and nervous?

6. Does it occur alone or in a flock?

7. In flying does it go:
 Straight and swift
 Dart about Up and down wave-like
 Flap the wings constantly
 Sail or soar with wings steady
 Flap the wings and then sail

8. Describe its song or call note?

9. Where does it sit when singing? Does it sing when flying?

14

FOR CLOSER OBSERVATION

10. Colors and markings of:

Breast: Top of head:

Wings: Eye streak:

Tail: Back:

11. Is the bill: Slender and long, short and thick, medium, curved, hooked?

12. Is the tail: Forked, notched, square, rounded?

THE FOLLOWING QUESTIONS SHOULD BE ANSWERED FROM OBSERVATION, IF POSSIBLE; IF NOT, THE ANSWER MAY BE FOUND BY CONSULTING BIRD BOOKS.

13. What is the food of the bird and how obtained?

14. Where does the bird spend the winter?

15. Describe the nest, where placed, how far from the ground, how supported, of what material is the outside made, how lined? The color and number of eggs.

16. How are the young fed and cared for? The colors of plumage of the young birds?

17. Is the bird beneficial to us, and if so, how and why?

UNDERSCORE THE WORDS WHICH DESCRIBE THE BIRD

Date:

Name of Bird: See Picture, page:

1. Where is the bird seen :

Woods	Open Field	Roadsides
Border of Woods	Trees	Border of Stream
Bushes	Along Fences	Marsh
About Buildings	Garden or Orchard	Pond or Lake

2. Compare the size of the bird with that of the crow, the robin, or the English Sparrow.

3. Its most striking colors are: Gray, slate, brown, chestnut, black, white, blue, red, yellow, orange, green, olive.

4. Does it show flash colors when flying? If so what color?
    Wing:
    Rump:
    Tail:
    Under Tail:

5. In action is it: Slow and quiet or active and nervous?

6. Does it occur alone or in a flock?

7. In flying does it go:
    Straight and swift
    Dart about Up and down wave-like
    Flap the wings constantly
    Sail or soar with wings steady
    Flap the wings and then sail

8. Describe its song or call note?

9. Where does it sit when singing? Does it sing when flying?

FOR CLOSER OBSERVATION

10. Colors and markings of:

Breast: Top of head:

Wings: Eye streak:

Tail: Back:

11. Is the bill: Slender and long, short and thick, medium, curved, hooked?

12. Is the tail: Forked, notched, square, rounded?

THE FOLLOWING QUESTIONS SHOULD BE ANSWERED FROM OBSERVATION, IF POSSIBLE; IF NOT, THE ANSWER MAY BE FOUND BY CONSULTING BIRD BOOKS.

13. What is the food of the bird and how obtained?

14. Where does the bird spend the winter?

15. Describe the nest, where placed, how far from the ground, how supported, of what material is the outside made, how lined? The color and number of eggs.

16. How are the young fed and cared for? The colors of plumage of the young birds?

17. Is the bird beneficial to us, and if so, how and why?

UNDERSCORE THE WORDS WHICH DESCRIBE THE BIRD

Date:

Name of Bird: See Picture, page:

1. Where is the bird seen :

Woods	Open Field	Roadsides
Border of Woods	Trees	Border of Stream
Bushes	Along Fences	Marsh
About Buildings	Garden or Orchard	Pond or Lake

2. Compare the size of the bird with that of the crow, the robin, or the English Sparrow.

3. Its most striking colors are: Gray, slate, brown, chestnut, black, white, blue, red, yellow, orange, green, olive.

4. Does it show flash colors when flying? If so what color?
    Wing:
    Rump:
    Tail:
    Under Tail:

5. In action is it: Slow and quiet or active and nervous?

6. Does it occur alone or in a flock?

7. In flying does it go:
    Straight and swift
    Dart about Up and down wave-like
    Flap the wings constantly
    Sail or soar with wings steady
    Flap the wings and then sail

8. Describe its song or call note?

9. Where does it sit when singing? Does it sing when flying?

FOR CLOSER OBSERVATION

10. Colors and markings of:

Breast: Top of head:

Wings: Eye streak:

Tail: Back:

11. Is the bill: Slender and long, short and thick, medium, curved, hooked?

12. Is the tail: Forked, notched, square, rounded?

THE FOLLOWING QUESTIONS SHOULD BE ANSWERED FROM OBSERVATION, IF POSSIBLE; IF NOT, THE ANSWER MAY BE FOUND BY CONSULTING BIRD BOOKS.

13. What is the food of the bird and how obtained?

14. Where does the bird spend the winter?

15. Describe the nest, where placed, how far from the ground, how supported, of what material is the outside made, how lined? The color and number of eggs.

16. How are the young fed and cared for? The colors of plumage of the young birds?

17. Is the bird beneficial to us, and if so, how and why?

UNDERSCORE THE WORDS WHICH DESCRIBE THE BIRD

Date:

Name of Bird: See Picture, page:

1. Where is the bird seen :

Woods	Open Field	Roadsides
Border of Woods	Trees	Border of Stream
Bushes	Along Fences	Marsh
About Buildings	Garden or Orchard	Pond or Lake

2. Compare the size of the bird with that of the crow, the robin, or the English Sparrow.

3. Its most striking colors are: Gray, slate, brown, chestnut, black, white, blue, red, yellow, orange, green, olive.

4. Does it show flash colors when flying? If so what color?
    Wing:
    Rump:
    Tail:
    Under Tail:

5. In action is it: Slow and quiet or active and nervous?

6. Does it occur alone or in a flock?

7. In flying does it go:
    Straight and swift
    Dart about Up and down wave-like
    Flap the wings constantly
    Sail or soar with wings steady
    Flap the wings and then sail

8. Describe its song or call note?

9. Where does it sit when singing? Does it sing when flying?

10. Colors and markings of:

Breast: Top of head:

Wings: Eye streak:

Tail: Back:

11. Is the bill: Slender and long, short and thick, medium, curved, hooked?

12. Is the tail: Forked, notched, square, rounded?

THE FOLLOWING QUESTIONS SHOULD BE ANSWERED FROM OBSERVATION, IF POSSIBLE; IF NOT, THE ANSWER MAY BE FOUND BY CONSULTING BIRD BOOKS.

13. What is the food of the bird and how obtained?

14. Where does the bird spend the winter?

15. Describe the nest, where placed, how far from the ground, how supported, of what material is the outside made, how lined? The color and number of eggs.

16. How are the young fed and cared for? The colors of plumage of the young birds?

17. Is the bird beneficial to us, and if so, how and why?

UNDERSCORE THE WORDS WHICH DESCRIBE THE BIRD

Date:

Name of Bird: See Picture, page:

1. Where is the bird seen :

Woods	Open Field	Roadsides
Border of Woods	Trees	Border of Stream
Bushes	Along Fences	Marsh
About Buildings	Garden or Orchard	Pond or Lake

2. Compare the size of the bird with that of the crow, the robin, or the English Sparrow.

3. Its most striking colors are: Gray, slate, brown, chestnut, black, white, blue, red, yellow, orange, green, olive.

4. Does it show flash colors when flying? If so what color?
    Wing:
    Rump:
    Tail:
    Under Tail:

5. In action is it: Slow and quiet or active and nervous?

6. Does it occur alone or in a flock?

7. In flying does it go:
    Straight and swift
    Dart about Up and down wave-like
    Flap the wings constantly
    Sail or soar with wings steady
    Flap the wings and then sail

8. Describe its song or call note?

9. Where does it sit when singing? Does it sing when flying?

FOR CLOSER OBSERVATION

10. Colors and markings of:

Breast: Top of head:

Wings: Eye streak:

Tail: Back:

11. Is the bill: Slender and long, short and thick, medium, curved, hooked?

12. Is the tail: Forked, notched, square, rounded?

THE FOLLOWING QUESTIONS SHOULD BE ANSWERED FROM OBSERVATION, IF POSSIBLE; IF NOT, THE ANSWER MAY BE FOUND BY CONSULTING BIRD BOOKS.

13. What is the food of the bird and how obtained?

14. Where does the bird spend the winter?

15. Describe the nest, where placed, how far from the ground, how supported, of what material is the outside made, how lined? The color and number of eggs.

16. How are the young fed and cared for? The colors of plumage of the young birds?

17. Is the bird beneficial to us, and if so, how and why?

UNDERSCORE THE WORDS WHICH DESCRIBE THE BIRD

Date:

Name of Bird: See Picture, page:

1. Where is the bird seen :

Woods	Open Field	Roadsides
Border of Woods	Trees	Border of Stream
Bushes	Along Fences	Marsh
About Buildings	Garden or Orchard	Pond or Lake

2. Compare the size of the bird with that of the crow, the robin, or the English Sparrow.

3. Its most striking colors are: Gray, slate, brown, chestnut, black, white, blue, red, yellow, orange, green, olive.

4. Does it show flash colors when flying? If so what color?
    Wing:
    Rump:
    Tail:
    Under Tail:

5. In action is it: Slow and quiet or active and nervous?

6. Does it occur alone or in a flock?

7. In flying does it go:
    Straight and swift
    Dart about Up and down wave-like
    Flap the wings constantly
    Sail or soar with wings steady
    Flap the wings and then sail

8. Describe its song or call note?

9. Where does it sit when singing? Does it sing when flying?

10. Colors and markings of:

Breast: Top of head:

Wings: Eye streak:

Tail: Back:

11. Is the bill: Slender and long, short and thick, medium, curved, hooked?

12. Is the tail: Forked, notched, square, rounded?

THE FOLLOWING QUESTIONS SHOULD BE ANSWERED FROM OBSERVATION, IF POSSIBLE; IF NOT, THE ANSWER MAY BE FOUND BY CONSULTING BIRD BOOKS.

13. What is the food of the bird and how obtained?

14. Where does the bird spend the winter?

15. Describe the nest, where placed, how far from the ground, how supported, of what material is the outside made, how lined? The color and number of eggs.

16. How are the young fed and cared for? The colors of plumage of the young birds?

17. Is the bird beneficial to us, and if so, how and why?

UNDERSCORE THE WORDS WHICH DESCRIBE THE BIRD

Date:

Name of Bird: See Picture, page:

1. Where is the bird seen :

Woods	Open Field	Roadsides
Border of Woods	Trees	Border of Stream
Bushes	Along Fences	Marsh
About Buildings	Garden or Orchard	Pond or Lake

2. Compare the size of the bird with that of the crow, the robin, or the English Sparrow.

3. Its most striking colors are: Gray, slate, brown, chestnut, black, white, blue, red, yellow, orange, green, olive.

4. Does it show flash colors when flying? If so what color?
    Wing:
    Rump:
    Tail:
    Under Tail:

5. In action is it: Slow and quiet or active and nervous?

6. Does it occur alone or in a flock?

7. In flying does it go:
    Straight and swift
    Dart about Up and down wave-like
    Flap the wings constantly
    Sail or soar with wings steady
    Flap the wings and then sail

8. Describe its song or call note?

9. Where does it sit when singing? Does it sing when flying?

FOR CLOSER OBSERVATION

10. Colors and markings of:

Breast: Top of head:

Wings: Eye streak:

Tail: Back:

11. Is the bill: Slender and long, short and thick, medium, curved, hooked?

12. Is the tail: Forked, notched, square, rounded?

THE FOLLOWING QUESTIONS SHOULD BE ANSWERED FROM OBSERVATION, IF POSSIBLE; IF NOT, THE ANSWER MAY BE FOUND BY CONSULTING BIRD BOOKS.

13. What is the food of the bird and how obtained?

14. Where does the bird spend the winter?

15. Describe the nest, where placed, how far from the ground, how supported, of what material is the outside made, how lined? The color and number of eggs.

16. How are the young fed and cared for? The colors of plumage of the young birds?

17. Is the bird beneficial to us, and if so, how and why?

UNDERSCORE THE WORDS WHICH DESCRIBE THE BIRD

Date:

Name of Bird: See Picture, page:

1. Where is the bird seen :

Woods	Open Field	Roadsides
Border of Woods	Trees	Border of Stream
Bushes	Along Fences	Marsh
About Buildings	Garden or Orchard	Pond or Lake

2. Compare the size of the bird with that of the crow, the robin, or the English Sparrow.

3. Its most striking colors are: Gray, slate, brown, chestnut, black, white, blue, red, yellow, orange, green, olive.

4. Does it show flash colors when flying? If so what color?
    Wing:
    Rump:
    Tail:
    Under Tail:

5. In action is it: Slow and quiet or active and nervous?

6. Does it occur alone or in a flock?

7. In flying does it go:
    Straight and swift
    Dart about Up and down wave-like
    Flap the wings constantly
    Sail or soar with wings steady
    Flap the wings and then sail

8. Describe its song or call note?

9. Where does it sit when singing? Does it sing when flying?

FOR CLOSER OBSERVATION

10. Colors and markings of:

Breast: Top of head:

Wings: Eye streak:

Tail: Back:

11. Is the bill: Slender and long, short and thick, medium, curved, hooked?

12. Is the tail: Forked, notched, square, rounded?

THE FOLLOWING QUESTIONS SHOULD BE ANSWERED FROM OBSERVATION, IF POSSIBLE; IF NOT, THE ANSWER MAY BE FOUND BY CONSULTING BIRD BOOKS.

13. What is the food of the bird and how obtained?

14. Where does the bird spend the winter?

15. Describe the nest, where placed, how far from the ground, how supported, of what material is the outside made, how lined? The color and number of eggs.

16. How are the young fed and cared for? The colors of plumage of the young birds?

17. Is the bird beneficial to us, and if so, how and why?

UNDERSCORE THE WORDS WHICH DESCRIBE THE BIRD

Date:

Name of Bird: See Picture, page:

1. Where is the bird seen :

Woods	Open Field	Roadsides
Border of Woods	Trees	Border of Stream
Bushes	Along Fences	Marsh
About Buildings	Garden or Orchard	Pond or Lake

2. Compare the size of the bird with that of the crow, the robin, or the English Sparrow.

3. Its most striking colors are: Gray, slate, brown, chestnut, black, white, blue, red, yellow, orange, green, olive.

4. Does it show flash colors when flying? If so what color?
    Wing:
    Rump:
    Tail:
    Under Tail:

5. In action is it: Slow and quiet or active and nervous?

6. Does it occur alone or in a flock?

7. In flying does it go:
    Straight and swift
    Dart about Up and down wave-like
    Flap the wings constantly
    Sail or soar with wings steady
    Flap the wings and then sail

8. Describe its song or call note?

9. Where does it sit when singing? Does it sing when flying?

FOR CLOSER OBSERVATION

10. Colors and markings of:

Breast: Top of head:

Wings: Eye streak:

Tail: Back:

11. Is the bill: Slender and long, short and thick, medium, curved, hooked?

12. Is the tail: Forked, notched, square, rounded?

THE FOLLOWING QUESTIONS SHOULD BE ANSWERED FROM OBSERVATION, IF POSSIBLE; IF NOT, THE ANSWER MAY BE FOUND BY CONSULTING BIRD BOOKS.

13. What is the food of the bird and how obtained?

14. Where does the bird spend the winter?

15. Describe the nest, where placed, how far from the ground, how supported, of what material is the outside made, how lined? The color and number of eggs.

16. How are the young fed and cared for? The colors of plumage of the young birds?

17. Is the bird beneficial to us, and if so, how and why?

UNDERSCORE THE WORDS WHICH DESCRIBE THE BIRD

Date:

Name of Bird: See Picture, page:

1. Where is the bird seen :

Woods	Open Field	Roadsides
Border of Woods	Trees	Border of Stream
Bushes	Along Fences	Marsh
About Buildings	Garden or Orchard	Pond or Lake

2. Compare the size of the bird with that of the crow, the robin, or the English Sparrow.

3. Its most striking colors are: Gray, slate, brown, chestnut, black, white, blue, red, yellow, orange, green, olive.

4. Does it show flash colors when flying? If so what color?
    Wing:
    Rump:
    Tail:
    Under Tail:

5. In action is it: Slow and quiet or active and nervous?

6. Does it occur alone or in a flock?

7. In flying does it go:
    Straight and swift
    Dart about Up and down wave-like
    Flap the wings constantly
    Sail or soar with wings steady
    Flap the wings and then sail

8. Describe its song or call note?

9. Where does it sit when singing? Does it sing when flying?

FOR CLOSER OBSERVATION

10. Colors and markings of:

Breast: Top of head:

Wings: Eye streak:

Tail: Back:

11. Is the bill: Slender and long, short and thick, medium, curved, hooked?

12. Is the tail: Forked, notched, square, rounded?

THE FOLLOWING QUESTIONS SHOULD BE ANSWERED FROM OBSERVATION, IF POSSIBLE; IF NOT, THE ANSWER MAY BE FOUND BY CONSULTING BIRD BOOKS.

13. What is the food of the bird and how obtained?

14. Where does the bird spend the winter?

15. Describe the nest, where placed, how far from the ground, how supported, of what material is the outside made, how lined? The color and number of eggs.

16. How are the young fed and cared for? The colors of plumage of the young birds?

17. Is the bird beneficial to us, and if so, how and why?

UNDERSCORE THE WORDS WHICH DESCRIBE THE BIRD

Date:

Name of Bird: See Picture, page:

1. Where is the bird seen :

Woods	Open Field	Roadsides
Border of Woods	Trees	Border of Stream
Bushes	Along Fences	Marsh
About Buildings	Garden or Orchard	Pond or Lake

2. Compare the size of the bird with that of the crow, the robin, or the English Sparrow.

3. Its most striking colors are: Gray, slate, brown, chestnut, black, white, blue, red, yellow, orange, green, olive.

4. Does it show flash colors when flying? If so what color?
   Wing:
   Rump:
   Tail:
   Under Tail:

5. In action is it: Slow and quiet or active and nervous?

6. Does it occur alone or in a flock?

7. In flying does it go:
   Straight and swift
   Dart about Up and down wave-like
   Flap the wings constantly
   Sail or soar with wings steady
   Flap the wings and then sail

8. Describe its song or call note?

9. Where does it sit when singing? Does it sing when flying?

FOR CLOSER OBSERVATION

10. Colors and markings of:

Breast: Top of head:

Wings: Eye streak:

Tail: Back:

11. Is the bill: Slender and long, short and thick, medium, curved, hooked?

12. Is the tail: Forked, notched, square, rounded?

THE FOLLOWING QUESTIONS SHOULD BE ANSWERED FROM OBSERVATION, IF POSSIBLE; IF NOT, THE ANSWER MAY BE FOUND BY CONSULTING BIRD BOOKS.

13. What is the food of the bird and how obtained?

14. Where does the bird spend the winter?

15. Describe the nest, where placed, how far from the ground, how supported, of what material is the outside made, how lined? The color and number of eggs.

16. How are the young fed and cared for? The colors of plumage of the young birds?

17. Is the bird beneficial to us, and if so, how and why?

UNDERSCORE THE WORDS WHICH DESCRIBE THE BIRD

Date:

Name of Bird: See Picture, page:

1. Where is the bird seen :

Woods	Open Field	Roadsides
Border of Woods	Trees	Border of Stream
Bushes	Along Fences	Marsh
About Buildings	Garden or Orchard	Pond or Lake

2. Compare the size of the bird with that of the crow, the robin, or the English Sparrow.

3. Its most striking colors are: Gray, slate, brown, chestnut, black, white, blue, red, yellow, orange, green, olive.

4. Does it show flash colors when flying? If so what color?
   Wing:
   Rump:
   Tail:
   Under Tail:

5. In action is it: Slow and quiet or active and nervous?

6. Does it occur alone or in a flock?

7. In flying does it go:
   Straight and swift
   Dart about Up and down wave-like
   Flap the wings constantly
   Sail or soar with wings steady
   Flap the wings and then sail

8. Describe its song or call note?

9. Where does it sit when singing? Does it sing when flying?

FOR CLOSER OBSERVATION

10. Colors and markings of:

Breast: Top of head:

Wings: Eye streak:

Tail: Back:

11. Is the bill: Slender and long, short and thick, medium, curved, hooked?

12. Is the tail: Forked, notched, square, rounded?

THE FOLLOWING QUESTIONS SHOULD BE ANSWERED FROM OBSERVATION, IF POSSIBLE; IF NOT, THE ANSWER MAY BE FOUND BY CONSULTING BIRD BOOKS.

13. What is the food of the bird and how obtained?

14. Where does the bird spend the winter?

15. Describe the nest, where placed, how far from the ground, how supported, of what material is the outside made, how lined? The color and number of eggs.

16. How are the young fed and cared for? The colors of plumage of the young birds?

17. Is the bird beneficial to us, and if so, how and why?

UNDERSCORE THE WORDS WHICH DESCRIBE THE BIRD

Date:

Name of Bird: See Picture, page:

1. Where is the bird seen :

Woods	Open Field	Roadsides
Border of Woods	Trees	Border of Stream
Bushes	Along Fences	Marsh
About Buildings	Garden or Orchard	Pond or Lake

2. Compare the size of the bird with that of the crow, the robin, or the English Sparrow.

3. Its most striking colors are: Gray, slate, brown, chestnut, black, white, blue, red, yellow, orange, green, olive.

4. Does it show flash colors when flying? If so what color?
    Wing:
    Rump:
    Tail:
    Under Tail:

5. In action is it: Slow and quiet or active and nervous?

6. Does it occur alone or in a flock?

7. In flying does it go:
    Straight and swift
    Dart about Up and down wave-like
    Flap the wings constantly
    Sail or soar with wings steady
    Flap the wings and then sail

8. Describe its song or call note?

9. Where does it sit when singing? Does it sing when flying?

FOR CLOSER OBSERVATION

10. Colors and markings of:

Breast: Top of head:

Wings: Eye streak:

Tail: Back:

11. Is the bill: Slender and long, short and thick, medium, curved, hooked?

12. Is the tail: Forked, notched, square, rounded?

THE FOLLOWING QUESTIONS SHOULD BE ANSWERED FROM OBSERVATION, IF POSSIBLE; IF NOT, THE ANSWER MAY BE FOUND BY CONSULTING BIRD BOOKS.

13. What is the food of the bird and how obtained?

14. Where does the bird spend the winter?

15. Describe the nest, where placed, how far from the ground, how supported, of what material is the outside made, how lined? The color and number of eggs.

16. How are the young fed and cared for? The colors of plumage of the young birds?

17. Is the bird beneficial to us, and if so, how and why?

UNDERSCORE THE WORDS WHICH DESCRIBE THE BIRD

Date:

Name of Bird: See Picture, page:

1. Where is the bird seen :

Woods	Open Field	Roadsides
Border of Woods	Trees	Border of Stream
Bushes	Along Fences	Marsh
About Buildings	Garden or Orchard	Pond or Lake

2. Compare the size of the bird with that of the crow, the robin, or the English Sparrow.

3. Its most striking colors are: Gray, slate, brown, chestnut, black, white, blue, red, yellow, orange, green, olive.

4. Does it show flash colors when flying? If so what color?
   Wing:
   Rump:
   Tail:
   Under Tail:

5. In action is it: Slow and quiet or active and nervous?

6. Does it occur alone or in a flock?

7. In flying does it go:
   Straight and swift
   Dart about Up and down wave-like
   Flap the wings constantly
   Sail or soar with wings steady
   Flap the wings and then sail

8. Describe its song or call note?

9. Where does it sit when singing? Does it sing when flying?

FOR CLOSER OBSERVATION

10. Colors and markings of:

Breast: Top of head:

Wings: Eye streak:

Tail: Back:

11. Is the bill: Slender and long, short and thick, medium, curved, hooked?

12. Is the tail: Forked, notched, square, rounded?

THE FOLLOWING QUESTIONS SHOULD BE ANSWERED FROM OBSERVATION, IF POSSIBLE; IF NOT, THE ANSWER MAY BE FOUND BY CONSULTING BIRD BOOKS.

13. What is the food of the bird and how obtained?

14. Where does the bird spend the winter?

15. Describe the nest, where placed, how far from the ground, how supported, of what material is the outside made, how lined? The color and number of eggs.

16. How are the young fed and cared for? The colors of plumage of the young birds?

17. Is the bird beneficial to us, and if so, how and why?

UNDERSCORE THE WORDS WHICH DESCRIBE THE BIRD

Date:

Name of Bird: See Picture, page:

1. Where is the bird seen :

Woods	Open Field	Roadsides
Border of Woods	Trees	Border of Stream
Bushes	Along Fences	Marsh
About Buildings	Garden or Orchard	Pond or Lake

2. Compare the size of the bird with that of the crow, the robin, or the English Sparrow.

3. Its most striking colors are: Gray, slate, brown, chestnut, black, white, blue, red, yellow, orange, green, olive.

4. Does it show flash colors when flying? If so what color?
   Wing:
   Rump:
   Tail:
   Under Tail:

5. In action is it: Slow and quiet or active and nervous?

6. Does it occur alone or in a flock?

7. In flying does it go:
   Straight and swift
   Dart about Up and down wave-like
   Flap the wings constantly
   Sail or soar with wings steady
   Flap the wings and then sail

8. Describe its song or call note?

9. Where does it sit when singing? Does it sing when flying?

FOR CLOSER OBSERVATION

10. Colors and markings of:

Breast: Top of head:

Wings: Eye streak:

Tail: Back:

11. Is the bill: Slender and long, short and thick, medium, curved, hooked?

12. Is the tail: Forked, notched, square, rounded?

THE FOLLOWING QUESTIONS SHOULD BE ANSWERED FROM OBSERVATION, IF POSSIBLE; IF NOT, THE ANSWER MAY BE FOUND BY CONSULTING BIRD BOOKS.

13. What is the food of the bird and how obtained?

14. Where does the bird spend the winter?

15. Describe the nest, where placed, how far from the ground, how supported, of what material is the outside made, how lined? The color and number of eggs.

16. How are the young fed and cared for? The colors of plumage of the young birds?

17. Is the bird beneficial to us, and if so, how and why?

UNDERSCORE THE WORDS WHICH DESCRIBE THE BIRD

Date:

Name of Bird: See Picture, page:

1. Where is the bird seen :

Woods	Open Field	Roadsides
Border of Woods	Trees	Border of Stream
Bushes	Along Fences	Marsh
About Buildings	Garden or Orchard	Pond or Lake

2. Compare the size of the bird with that of the crow, the robin, or the English Sparrow.

3. Its most striking colors are: Gray, slate, brown, chestnut, black, white, blue, red, yellow, orange, green, olive.

4. Does it show flash colors when flying? If so what color?
    Wing:
    Rump:
    Tail:
    Under Tail:

5. In action is it: Slow and quiet or active and nervous?

6. Does it occur alone or in a flock?

7. In flying does it go:
    Straight and swift
    Dart about Up and down wave-like
    Flap the wings constantly
    Sail or soar with wings steady
    Flap the wings and then sail

8. Describe its song or call note?

9. Where does it sit when singing? Does it sing when flying?

FOR CLOSER OBSERVATION

10. Colors and markings of:

Breast: Top of head:

Wings: Eye streak:

Tail: Back:

11. Is the bill: Slender and long, short and thick, medium, curved, hooked?

12. Is the tail: Forked, notched, square, rounded?

THE FOLLOWING QUESTIONS SHOULD BE ANSWERED FROM OBSERVATION, IF POSSIBLE; IF NOT, THE ANSWER MAY BE FOUND BY CONSULTING BIRD BOOKS.

13. What is the food of the bird and how obtained?

14. Where does the bird spend the winter?

15. Describe the nest, where placed, how far from the ground, how supported, of what material is the outside made, how lined? The color and number of eggs.

16. How are the young fed and cared for? The colors of plumage of the young birds?

17. Is the bird beneficial to us, and if so, how and why?

UNDERSCORE THE WORDS WHICH DESCRIBE THE BIRD

Date:

Name of Bird: See Picture, page:

1. Where is the bird seen :

Woods	Open Field	Roadsides
Border of Woods	Trees	Border of Stream
Bushes	Along Fences	Marsh
About Buildings	Garden or Orchard	Pond or Lake

2. Compare the size of the bird with that of the crow, the robin, or the English Sparrow.

3. Its most striking colors are: Gray, slate, brown, chestnut, black, white, blue, red, yellow, orange, green, olive.

4. Does it show flash colors when flying? If so what color?
   Wing:
   Rump:
   Tail:
   Under Tail:

5. In action is it: Slow and quiet or active and nervous?

6. Does it occur alone or in a flock?

7. In flying does it go:
   Straight and swift
   Dart about Up and down wave-like
   Flap the wings constantly
   Sail or soar with wings steady
   Flap the wings and then sail

8. Describe its song or call note?

9. Where does it sit when singing? Does it sing when flying?

10. Colors and markings of:

Breast: Top of head:

Wings: Eye streak:

Tail: Back:

11. Is the bill: Slender and long, short and thick, medium, curved, hooked?

12. Is the tail: Forked, notched, square, rounded?

THE FOLLOWING QUESTIONS SHOULD BE ANSWERED FROM OBSERVATION, IF POSSIBLE; IF NOT, THE ANSWER MAY BE FOUND BY CONSULTING BIRD BOOKS.

13. What is the food of the bird and how obtained?

14. Where does the bird spend the winter?

15. Describe the nest, where placed, how far from the ground, how supported, of what material is the outside made, how lined? The color and number of eggs.

16. How are the young fed and cared for? The colors of plumage of the young birds?

17. Is the bird beneficial to us, and if so, how and why?

UNDERSCORE THE WORDS WHICH DESCRIBE THE BIRD

Date:

Name of Bird: See Picture, page:

1. Where is the bird seen :

Woods	Open Field	Roadsides
Border of Woods	Trees	Border of Stream
Bushes	Along Fences	Marsh
About Buildings	Garden or Orchard	Pond or Lake

2. Compare the size of the bird with that of the crow, the robin, or the English Sparrow.

3. Its most striking colors are: Gray, slate, brown, chestnut, black, white, blue, red, yellow, orange, green, olive.

4. Does it show flash colors when flying? If so what color?
    Wing:
    Rump:
    Tail:
    Under Tail:

5. In action is it: Slow and quiet or active and nervous?

6. Does it occur alone or in a flock?

7. In flying does it go:
    Straight and swift
    Dart about Up and down wave-like
    Flap the wings constantly
    Sail or soar with wings steady
    Flap the wings and then sail

8. Describe its song or call note?

9. Where does it sit when singing? Does it sing when flying?

FOR CLOSER OBSERVATION

10. Colors and markings of:

Breast: Top of head:

Wings: Eye streak:

Tail: Back:

11. Is the bill: Slender and long, short and thick, medium, curved, hooked?

12. Is the tail: Forked, notched, square, rounded?

THE FOLLOWING QUESTIONS SHOULD BE ANSWERED FROM OBSERVATION, IF POSSIBLE; IF NOT, THE ANSWER MAY BE FOUND BY CONSULTING BIRD BOOKS.

13. What is the food of the bird and how obtained?

14. Where does the bird spend the winter?

15. Describe the nest, where placed, how far from the ground, how supported, of what material is the outside made, how lined? The color and number of eggs.

16. How are the young fed and cared for? The colors of plumage of the young birds?

17. Is the bird beneficial to us, and if so, how and why?

UNDERSCORE THE WORDS WHICH DESCRIBE THE BIRD

Date:

Name of Bird: See Picture, page:

1. Where is the bird seen :

Woods	Open Field	Roadsides
Border of Woods	Trees	Border of Stream
Bushes	Along Fences	Marsh
About Buildings	Garden or Orchard	Pond or Lake

2. Compare the size of the bird with that of the crow, the robin, or the English Sparrow.

3. Its most striking colors are: Gray, slate, brown, chestnut, black, white, blue, red, yellow, orange, green, olive.

4. Does it show flash colors when flying? If so what color?
    Wing:
    Rump:
    Tail:
    Under Tail:

5. In action is it: Slow and quiet or active and nervous?

6. Does it occur alone or in a flock?

7. In flying does it go:
    Straight and swift
    Dart about Up and down wave-like
    Flap the wings constantly
    Sail or soar with wings steady
    Flap the wings and then sail

8. Describe its song or call note?

9. Where does it sit when singing? Does it sing when flying?

FOR CLOSER OBSERVATION

10. Colors and markings of:

Breast: Top of head:

Wings: Eye streak:

Tail: Back:

11. Is the bill: Slender and long, short and thick, medium, curved, hooked?

12. Is the tail: Forked, notched, square, rounded?

THE FOLLOWING QUESTIONS SHOULD BE ANSWERED FROM OBSERVATION, IF POSSIBLE; IF NOT, THE ANSWER MAY BE FOUND BY CONSULTING BIRD BOOKS.

13. What is the food of the bird and how obtained?

14. Where does the bird spend the winter?

15. Describe the nest, where placed, how far from the ground, how supported, of what material is the outside made, how lined? The color and number of eggs.

16. How are the young fed and cared for? The colors of plumage of the young birds?

17. Is the bird beneficial to us, and if so, how and why?

UNDERSCORE THE WORDS WHICH DESCRIBE THE BIRD

Date:

Name of Bird: See Picture, page:

1. Where is the bird seen :

Woods	Open Field	Roadsides
Border of Woods	Trees	Border of Stream
Bushes	Along Fences	Marsh
About Buildings	Garden or Orchard	Pond or Lake

2. Compare the size of the bird with that of the crow, the robin, or the English Sparrow.

3. Its most striking colors are: Gray, slate, brown, chestnut, black, white, blue, red, yellow, orange, green, olive.

4. Does it show flash colors when flying? If so what color?
    Wing:
    Rump:
    Tail:
    Under Tail:

5. In action is it: Slow and quiet or active and nervous?

6. Does it occur alone or in a flock?

7. In flying does it go:
    Straight and swift
    Dart about Up and down wave-like
    Flap the wings constantly
    Sail or soar with wings steady
    Flap the wings and then sail

8. Describe its song or call note?

9. Where does it sit when singing? Does it sing when flying?

FOR CLOSER OBSERVATION

10. Colors and markings of:

Breast: Top of head:

Wings: Eye streak:

Tail: Back:

11. Is the bill: Slender and long, short and thick, medium, curved, hooked?

12. Is the tail: Forked, notched, square, rounded?

THE FOLLOWING QUESTIONS SHOULD BE ANSWERED FROM OBSERVATION, IF POSSIBLE; IF NOT, THE ANSWER MAY BE FOUND BY CONSULTING BIRD BOOKS.

13. What is the food of the bird and how obtained?

14. Where does the bird spend the winter?

15. Describe the nest, where placed, how far from the ground, how supported, of what material is the outside made, how lined? The color and number of eggs.

16. How are the young fed and cared for? The colors of plumage of the young birds?

17. Is the bird beneficial to us, and if so, how and why?

UNDERSCORE THE WORDS WHICH DESCRIBE THE BIRD

Date:

Name of Bird: See Picture, page:

1. Where is the bird seen :

Woods   Open Field   Roadsides
Border of Woods   Trees   Border of Stream
Bushes   Along Fences   Marsh
About Buildings   Garden or Orchard   Pond or Lake

2. Compare the size of the bird with that of the crow, the robin, or the English Sparrow.

3. Its most striking colors are: Gray, slate, brown, chestnut, black, white, blue, red, yellow, orange, green, olive.

4. Does it show flash colors when flying? If so what color?
    Wing:
    Rump:
    Tail:
    Under Tail:

5. In action is it: Slow and quiet or active and nervous?

6. Does it occur alone or in a flock?

7. In flying does it go:
    Straight and swift
    Dart about Up and down wave-like
    Flap the wings constantly
    Sail or soar with wings steady
    Flap the wings and then sail

8. Describe its song or call note?

9. Where does it sit when singing? Does it sing when flying?

54

FOR CLOSER OBSERVATION

10. Colors and markings of:

Breast: Top of head:

Wings: Eye streak:

Tail: Back:

11. Is the bill: Slender and long, short and thick, medium, curved, hooked?

12. Is the tail: Forked, notched, square, rounded?

THE FOLLOWING QUESTIONS SHOULD BE ANSWERED FROM OBSERVATION, IF POSSIBLE; IF NOT, THE ANSWER MAY BE FOUND BY CONSULTING BIRD BOOKS.

13. What is the food of the bird and how obtained?

14. Where does the bird spend the winter?

15. Describe the nest, where placed, how far from the ground, how supported, of what material is the outside made, how lined? The color and number of eggs.

16. How are the young fed and cared for? The colors of plumage of the young birds?

17. Is the bird beneficial to us, and if so, how and why?

UNDERSCORE THE WORDS WHICH DESCRIBE THE BIRD

Date:

Name of Bird: See Picture, page:

1. Where is the bird seen :

Woods	Open Field	Roadsides
Border of Woods	Trees	Border of Stream
Bushes	Along Fences	Marsh
About Buildings	Garden or Orchard	Pond or Lake

2. Compare the size of the bird with that of the crow, the robin, or the English Sparrow.

3. Its most striking colors are: Gray, slate, brown, chestnut, black, white, blue, red, yellow, orange, green, olive.

4. Does it show flash colors when flying? If so what color?
   Wing:
   Rump:
   Tail:
   Under Tail:

5. In action is it: Slow and quiet or active and nervous?

6. Does it occur alone or in a flock?

7. In flying does it go:
   Straight and swift
   Dart about Up and down wave-like
   Flap the wings constantly
   Sail or soar with wings steady
   Flap the wings and then sail

8. Describe its song or call note?

9. Where does it sit when singing? Does it sing when flying?

FOR CLOSER OBSERVATION

10. Colors and markings of:

Breast: Top of head:

Wings: Eye streak:

Tail: Back:

11. Is the bill: Slender and long, short and thick, medium, curved, hooked?

12. Is the tail: Forked, notched, square, rounded?

THE FOLLOWING QUESTIONS SHOULD BE ANSWERED FROM OBSERVATION, IF POSSIBLE; IF NOT, THE ANSWER MAY BE FOUND BY CONSULTING BIRD BOOKS.

13. What is the food of the bird and how obtained?

14. Where does the bird spend the winter?

15. Describe the nest, where placed, how far from the ground, how supported, of what material is the outside made, how lined? The color and number of eggs.

16. How are the young fed and cared for? The colors of plumage of the young birds?

17. Is the bird beneficial to us, and if so, how and why?

UNDERSCORE THE WORDS WHICH DESCRIBE THE BIRD

Date:

Name of Bird: See Picture, page:

1. Where is the bird seen :

Woods	Open Field	Roadsides
Border of Woods	Trees	Border of Stream
Bushes	Along Fences	Marsh
About Buildings	Garden or Orchard	Pond or Lake

2. Compare the size of the bird with that of the crow, the robin, or the English Sparrow.

3. Its most striking colors are: Gray, slate, brown, chestnut, black, white, blue, red, yellow, orange, green, olive.

4. Does it show flash colors when flying? If so what color?
    Wing:
    Rump:
    Tail:
    Under Tail:

5. In action is it: Slow and quiet or active and nervous?

6. Does it occur alone or in a flock?

7. In flying does it go:
    Straight and swift
    Dart about Up and down wave-like
    Flap the wings constantly
    Sail or soar with wings steady
    Flap the wings and then sail

8. Describe its song or call note?

9. Where does it sit when singing? Does it sing when flying?

FOR CLOSER OBSERVATION

10. Colors and markings of:

Breast: Top of head:

Wings: Eye streak:

Tail: Back:

11. Is the bill: Slender and long, short and thick, medium, curved, hooked?

12. Is the tail: Forked, notched, square, rounded?

THE FOLLOWING QUESTIONS SHOULD BE ANSWERED FROM OBSERVATION, IF POSSIBLE; IF NOT, THE ANSWER MAY BE FOUND BY CONSULTING BIRD BOOKS.

13. What is the food of the bird and how obtained?

14. Where does the bird spend the winter?

15. Describe the nest, where placed, how far from the ground, how supported, of what material is the outside made, how lined? The color and number of eggs.

16. How are the young fed and cared for? The colors of plumage of the young birds?

17. Is the bird beneficial to us, and if so, how and why?

UNDERSCORE THE WORDS WHICH DESCRIBE THE BIRD

Date:

Name of Bird: See Picture, page:

1. Where is the bird seen :

Woods	Open Field	Roadsides
Border of Woods	Trees	Border of Stream
Bushes	Along Fences	Marsh
About Buildings	Garden or Orchard	Pond or Lake

2. Compare the size of the bird with that of the crow, the robin, or the English Sparrow.

3. Its most striking colors are: Gray, slate, brown, chestnut, black, white, blue, red, yellow, orange, green, olive.

4. Does it show flash colors when flying? If so what color?
   Wing:
   Rump:
   Tail:
   Under Tail:

5. In action is it: Slow and quiet or active and nervous?

6. Does it occur alone or in a flock?

7. In flying does it go:
   Straight and swift
   Dart about Up and down wave-like
   Flap the wings constantly
   Sail or soar with wings steady
   Flap the wings and then sail

8. Describe its song or call note?

9. Where does it sit when singing? Does it sing when flying?

FOR CLOSER OBSERVATION

10. Colors and markings of:

Breast: Top of head:

Wings: Eye streak:

Tail: Back:

11. Is the bill: Slender and long, short and thick, medium, curved, hooked?

12. Is the tail: Forked, notched, square, rounded?

THE FOLLOWING QUESTIONS SHOULD BE ANSWERED FROM OBSERVATION, IF POSSIBLE; IF NOT, THE ANSWER MAY BE FOUND BY CONSULTING BIRD BOOKS.

13. What is the food of the bird and how obtained?

14. Where does the bird spend the winter?

15. Describe the nest, where placed, how far from the ground, how supported, of what material is the outside made, how lined? The color and number of eggs.

16. How are the young fed and cared for? The colors of plumage of the young birds?

17. Is the bird beneficial to us, and if so, how and why?

UNDERSCORE THE WORDS WHICH DESCRIBE THE BIRD

Date:

Name of Bird: See Picture, page:

1. Where is the bird seen :

Woods	Open Field	Roadsides
Border of Woods	Trees	Border of Stream
Bushes	Along Fences	Marsh
About Buildings	Garden or Orchard	Pond or Lake

2. Compare the size of the bird with that of the crow, the robin, or the English Sparrow.

3. Its most striking colors are: Gray, slate, brown, chestnut, black, white, blue, red, yellow, orange, green, olive.

4. Does it show flash colors when flying? If so what color?
    Wing:
    Rump:
    Tail:
    Under Tail:

5. In action is it: Slow and quiet or active and nervous?

6. Does it occur alone or in a flock?

7. In flying does it go:
    Straight and swift
    Dart about Up and down wave-like
    Flap the wings constantly
    Sail or soar with wings steady
    Flap the wings and then sail

8. Describe its song or call note?

9. Where does it sit when singing? Does it sing when flying?

FOR CLOSER OBSERVATION

10. Colors and markings of:

Breast: Top of head:

Wings: Eye streak:

Tail: Back:

11. Is the bill: Slender and long, short and thick, medium, curved, hooked?

12. Is the tail: Forked, notched, square, rounded?

THE FOLLOWING QUESTIONS SHOULD BE ANSWERED FROM OBSERVATION, IF POSSIBLE; IF NOT, THE ANSWER MAY BE FOUND BY CONSULTING BIRD BOOKS.

13. What is the food of the bird and how obtained?

14. Where does the bird spend the winter?

15. Describe the nest, where placed, how far from the ground, how supported, of what material is the outside made, how lined? The color and number of eggs.

16. How are the young fed and cared for? The colors of plumage of the young birds?

17. Is the bird beneficial to us, and if so, how and why?

UNDERSCORE THE WORDS WHICH DESCRIBE THE BIRD

Date:

Name of Bird: See Picture, page:

1. Where is the bird seen :

Woods	Open Field	Roadsides
Border of Woods	Trees	Border of Stream
Bushes	Along Fences	Marsh
About Buildings	Garden or Orchard	Pond or Lake

2. Compare the size of the bird with that of the crow, the robin, or the English Sparrow.

3. Its most striking colors are: Gray, slate, brown, chestnut, black, white, blue, red, yellow, orange, green, olive.

4. Does it show flash colors when flying? If so what color?
    Wing:
    Rump:
    Tail:
    Under Tail:

5. In action is it: Slow and quiet or active and nervous?

6. Does it occur alone or in a flock?

7. In flying does it go:
    Straight and swift
    Dart about Up and down wave-like
    Flap the wings constantly
    Sail or soar with wings steady
    Flap the wings and then sail

8. Describe its song or call note?

9. Where does it sit when singing? Does it sing when flying?

FOR CLOSER OBSERVATION

10. Colors and markings of:

Breast: Top of head:

Wings: Eye streak:

Tail: Back:

11. Is the bill: Slender and long, short and thick, medium, curved, hooked?

12. Is the tail: Forked, notched, square, rounded?

THE FOLLOWING QUESTIONS SHOULD BE ANSWERED FROM OBSERVATION, IF POSSIBLE; IF NOT, THE ANSWER MAY BE FOUND BY CONSULTING BIRD BOOKS.

13. What is the food of the bird and how obtained?

14. Where does the bird spend the winter?

15. Describe the nest, where placed, how far from the ground, how supported, of what material is the outside made, how lined? The color and number of eggs.

16. How are the young fed and cared for? The colors of plumage of the young birds?

17. Is the bird beneficial to us, and if so, how and why?

UNDERSCORE THE WORDS WHICH DESCRIBE THE BIRD

Date:

Name of Bird: See Picture, page:

1. Where is the bird seen :

Woods	Open Field	Roadsides
Border of Woods	Trees	Border of Stream
Bushes	Along Fences	Marsh
About Buildings	Garden or Orchard	Pond or Lake

2. Compare the size of the bird with that of the crow, the robin, or the English Sparrow.

3. Its most striking colors are: Gray, slate, brown, chestnut, black, white, blue, red, yellow, orange, green, olive.

4. Does it show flash colors when flying? If so what color?
   Wing:
   Rump:
   Tail:
   Under Tail:

5. In action is it: Slow and quiet or active and nervous?

6. Does it occur alone or in a flock?

7. In flying does it go:
   Straight and swift
   Dart about Up and down wave-like
   Flap the wings constantly
   Sail or soar with wings steady
   Flap the wings and then sail

8. Describe its song or call note?

9. Where does it sit when singing? Does it sing when flying?

FOR CLOSER OBSERVATION

10. Colors and markings of:

Breast: Top of head:

Wings: Eye streak:

Tail: Back:

11. Is the bill: Slender and long, short and thick, medium, curved, hooked?

12. Is the tail: Forked, notched, square, rounded?

THE FOLLOWING QUESTIONS SHOULD BE ANSWERED FROM OBSERVATION, IF POSSIBLE; IF NOT, THE ANSWER MAY BE FOUND BY CONSULTING BIRD BOOKS.

13. What is the food of the bird and how obtained?

14. Where does the bird spend the winter?

15. Describe the nest, where placed, how far from the ground, how supported, of what material is the outside made, how lined? The color and number of eggs.

16. How are the young fed and cared for? The colors of plumage of the young birds?

17. Is the bird beneficial to us, and if so, how and why?

UNDERSCORE THE WORDS WHICH DESCRIBE THE BIRD

Date:

Name of Bird: See Picture, page:

1. Where is the bird seen :

Woods	Open Field	Roadsides
Border of Woods	Trees	Border of Stream
Bushes	Along Fences	Marsh
About Buildings	Garden or Orchard	Pond or Lake

2. Compare the size of the bird with that of the crow, the robin, or the English Sparrow.

3. Its most striking colors are: Gray, slate, brown, chestnut, black, white, blue, red, yellow, orange, green, olive.

4. Does it show flash colors when flying? If so what color?
    Wing:
    Rump:
    Tail:
    Under Tail:

5. In action is it: Slow and quiet or active and nervous?

6. Does it occur alone or in a flock?

7. In flying does it go:
    Straight and swift
    Dart about Up and down wave-like
    Flap the wings constantly
    Sail or soar with wings steady
    Flap the wings and then sail

8. Describe its song or call note?

9. Where does it sit when singing? Does it sing when flying?

10. Colors and markings of:

Breast: Top of head:

Wings: Eye streak:

Tail: Back:

11. Is the bill: Slender and long, short and thick, medium, curved, hooked?

12. Is the tail: Forked, notched, square, rounded?

THE FOLLOWING QUESTIONS SHOULD BE ANSWERED FROM OBSERVATION, IF POSSIBLE; IF NOT, THE ANSWER MAY BE FOUND BY CONSULTING BIRD BOOKS.

13. What is the food of the bird and how obtained?

14. Where does the bird spend the winter?

15. Describe the nest, where placed, how far from the ground, how supported, of what material is the outside made, how lined? The color and number of eggs.

16. How are the young fed and cared for? The colors of plumage of the young birds?

17. Is the bird beneficial to us, and if so, how and why?

UNDERSCORE THE WORDS WHICH DESCRIBE THE BIRD

Date:

Name of Bird: See Picture, page:

1. Where is the bird seen :

Woods	Open Field	Roadsides
Border of Woods	Trees	Border of Stream
Bushes	Along Fences	Marsh
About Buildings	Garden or Orchard	Pond or Lake

2. Compare the size of the bird with that of the crow, the robin, or the English Sparrow.

3. Its most striking colors are: Gray, slate, brown, chestnut, black, white, blue, red, yellow, orange, green, olive.

4. Does it show flash colors when flying? If so what color?
    Wing:
    Rump:
    Tail:
    Under Tail:

5. In action is it: Slow and quiet or active and nervous?

6. Does it occur alone or in a flock?

7. In flying does it go:
    Straight and swift
    Dart about Up and down wave-like
    Flap the wings constantly
    Sail or soar with wings steady
    Flap the wings and then sail

8. Describe its song or call note?

9. Where does it sit when singing? Does it sing when flying?

FOR CLOSER OBSERVATION

10. Colors and markings of:

Breast: Top of head:

Wings: Eye streak:

Tail: Back:

11. Is the bill: Slender and long, short and thick, medium, curved, hooked?

12. Is the tail: Forked, notched, square, rounded?

THE FOLLOWING QUESTIONS SHOULD BE ANSWERED FROM OBSERVATION, IF POSSIBLE; IF NOT, THE ANSWER MAY BE FOUND BY CONSULTING BIRD BOOKS.

13. What is the food of the bird and how obtained?

14. Where does the bird spend the winter?

15. Describe the nest, where placed, how far from the ground, how supported, of what material is the outside made, how lined? The color and number of eggs.

16. How are the young fed and cared for? The colors of plumage of the young birds?

17. Is the bird beneficial to us, and if so, how and why?

INDEX TO PICTURES

The Bluebird

Plate 1.

See Page_____

The Robin

Plate 2.

See Page_____

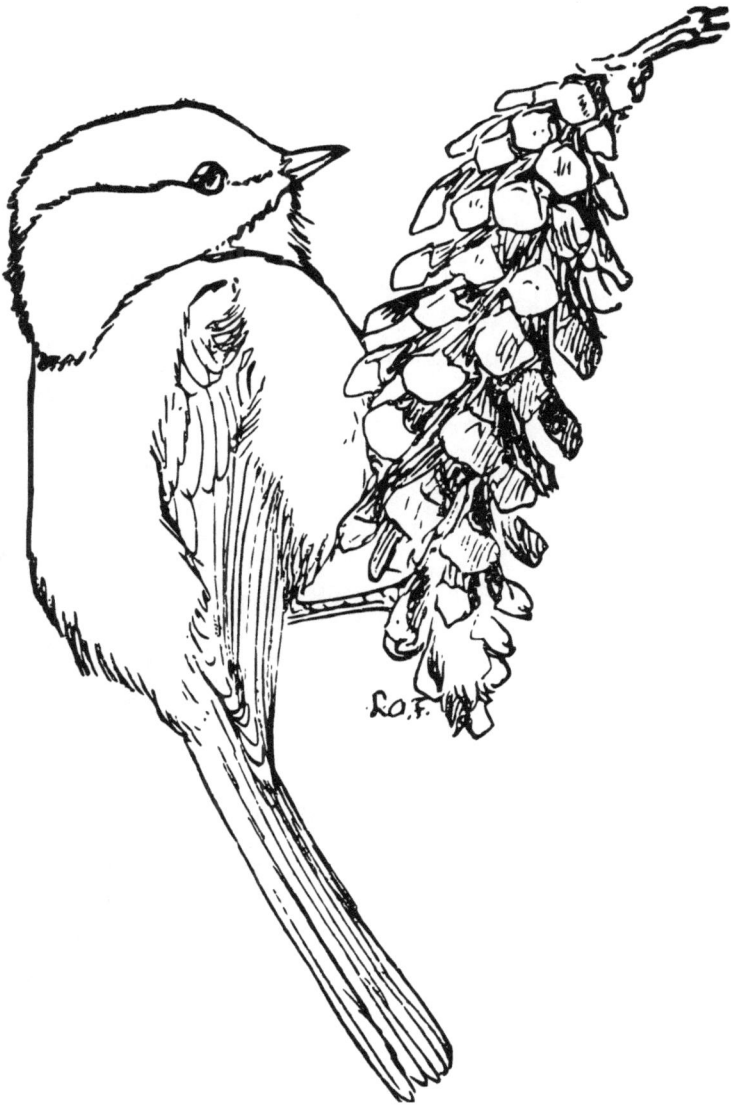

The Chick-a-dee

Plate 3.

See Page_____

The White-breasted Nuthatch

Plate 4.

See Page_____

The Brown Creeper

Plate 5.

*See Page*_____

The House Wren

Plate 6.

See Page_____

The Brown Thrasher

Plate 7.

See Page_____

The Catbird

Plate 8.

See Page_____

The Mockingbird

Plate 9.

See Page_____

1. The Purple Martin
Shining blue black wings and wings and tail duller

2. Eave or Cliff Swallow
Back and crown steel blue, forehead cream white, thorat and sides od head
chesnut, beast brownish gray, underparts whiteish

3. Sandbank Swallow
Upper parts and band on breast brownish gray, throat and underparts white

4. Barn Swallow
Upper parts dark blue, forhead, throat and breast reddish brown

5. Tree Swallow
Upper parts dark blue or green throat and underparts white

Plate 10.

See Page_____

The Rose -breasted Grosbeak

Plate 11.

See Page_____

The Song Sparrow

Plate 12.

*See Page*_____

The Chipping Sparrow Or "Chippy"

Plate 13.

See Page_____

The English Sparow

Plate 14.

See Page_____

The Red-winged Blackbird

Plate 15.

See Page_____

The Bobolink

Plate 16.

See Page_____

The Baltimore Oriole

Plate 17.

*See Page*_____

The Meadowlark

Plate 18.

See Page_____

The Horned Lark

Plate 19.

See Page_____

The Bluejay

Plate 20.

See Page_____

The Kingbird

Plate 21.

See Page_____

The Downy Woodpecker

Plate 22.

See Page_____

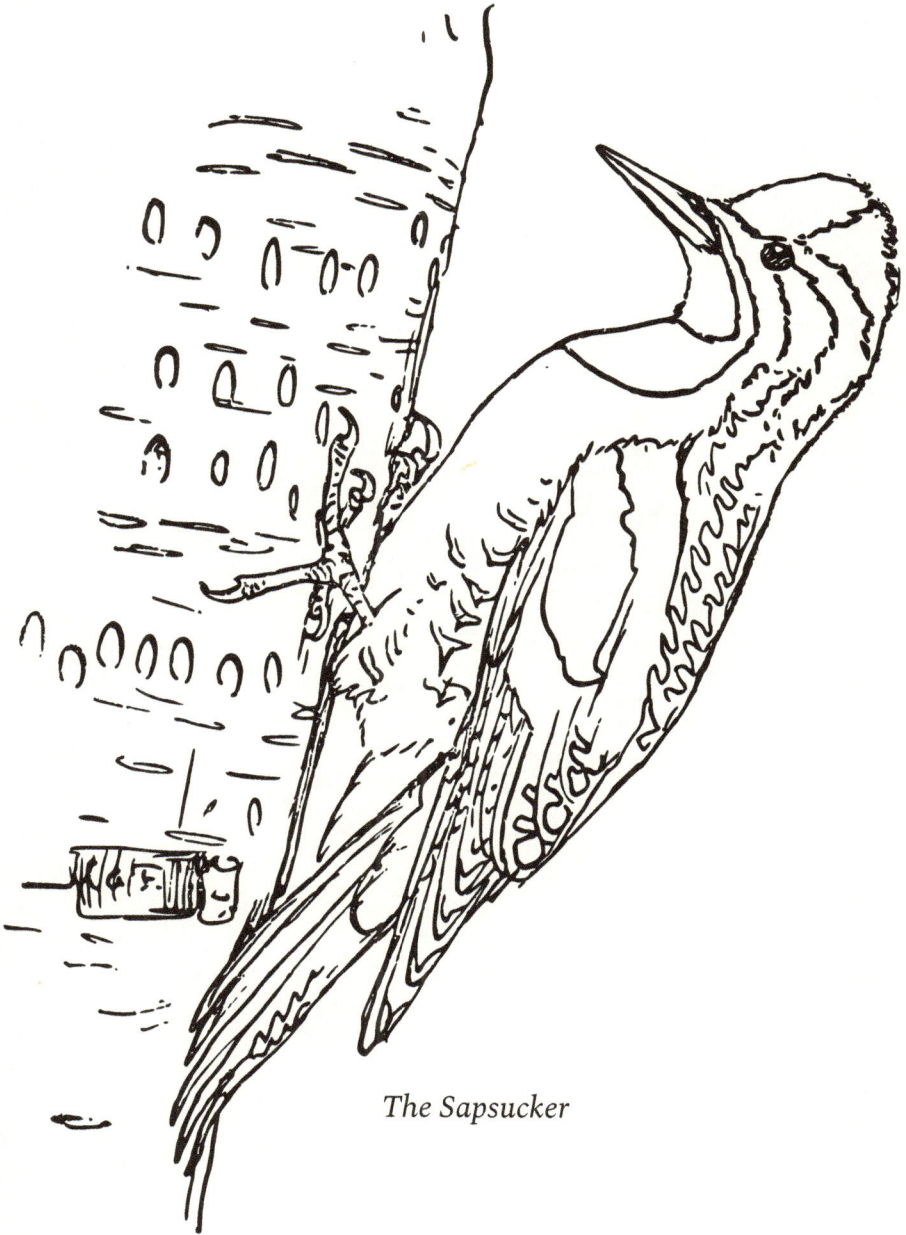

119

The Sapsucker

Plate 23.

See Page_____

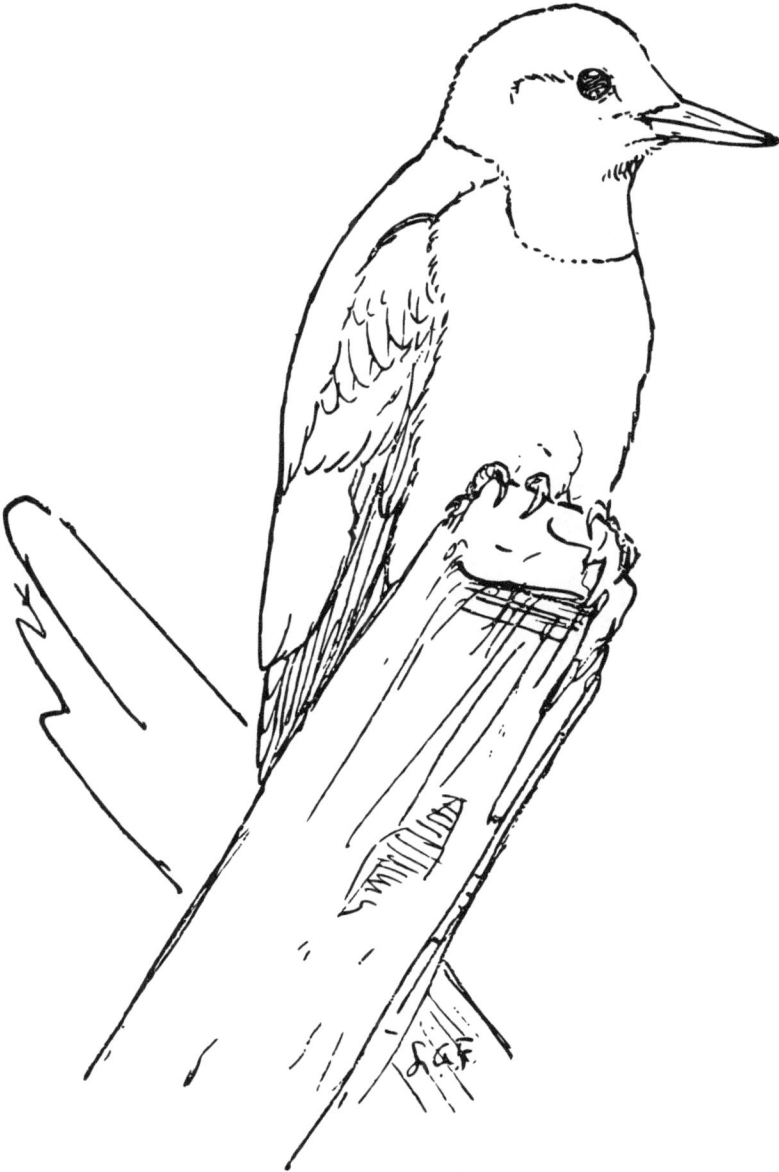

The Red-headed Woodpecker

Plate 24.

See Page_____

The Flicker

Plate 25.

See Page_____

The Bobwhite

Plate 26.

See Page_____

www.ingramcontent.com/pod-product-compliance
Lightning Source LLC
Chambersburg PA
CBHW022100020426
42335CB00012B/771